CONTENTS

GENERAL LEARNING OBJECTIVES OF THIS UNIT

This Open Learning Unit will supply you with all the core information you need to answer an examination question or to write an essay on thinking and problem solving. It is likely that it will take you about four hours to work through, though if you undertake all the suggested activities it might well take longer.

By the end of this Unit you should:

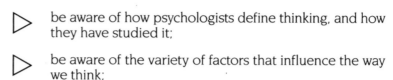 be aware of how psychologists define thinking, and how they have studied it;

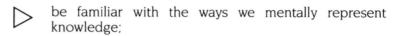 be aware of the variety of factors that influence the way we think;

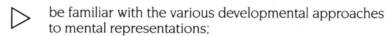 be familiar with the ways we mentally represent knowledge;

be familiar with the various developmental approaches to mental representations;

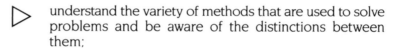 understand the variety of methods that are used to solve problems and be aware of the distinctions between them;

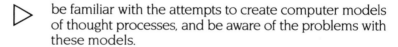 be familiar with the attempts to create computer models of thought processes, and be aware of the problems with these models.

Defining Thinking

KEY AIMS: By the end of Part 1 you should:

▷ *have a basic understanding of the issues around the study of thinking, and use this information to reflect on your own experience*

▷ *understand the various approaches taken by psychologists towards thinking*

▷ *attempt to be critical of these approaches.*

'What are you thinking about? You look miles away.'

Coming back to my senses I realize that I have not been paying attention* to what is happening around me. Someone has been speaking to me and I've been thinking* about something else.

Embarrassing episodes like this are very common. But if truth be known, whenever someone talks to me, I am thinking at the same time, often about something quite different. Sometimes that train of thought takes over and I start to pay less attention to the conversation that I'm supposed to be having. Then I have an embarrassing moment like the one described above.

SOMETHING TO TRY

I'll think about it. *You think about things too much.*
I think I love you. *Think about it.*
I think therefore I am. *I think I can.*

These are some examples of everyday phrases that refer to thinking. Write down other uses of the term 'thinking'.

All our waking life, something is going on in our minds. We are thinking. But, what are we thinking about, and how do we think?

SOMETHING TO TRY

Try to think about your thoughts.
What have you just been thinking about?
How were you thinking?
Did you think in words?
Was it a conversation, if so, who with?
Did you have a mental audience? For example, were you imagining your mother watching and listening to you?
Did you think in pictures?
Were you able to control the pictures fully or did they sometimes change without you wanting them to?
Why were you thinking about that?

Tough questions. If you think about them too much you'll end up with a headache! Psychology has tried to study this puzzling process of thinking. Like a number of psychological processes, we do it so naturally that it is rather hard to describe how we do it. The more we take something for granted, the harder it is to explain. To take an everyday example of a physical skill, it is very hard for a good swimmer to explain to a non swimmer how to swim.

FIGURE 1. *The dying fly.*

Table 1: FIVE DIFFERENT APPROACHES TO THINKING

1. Thinking as association of ideas
2. Thinking as response to biological demands
3. Thinking as adaptation to the environment
4. Thinking as cognitive restructuring (figuring it out)
5. Thinking as resolving discrepancies

Thinking as association

Perhaps one of the earliest models of thought which was adopted in psychology came from the work of the philosopher John Locke, who lived in the 17th century. Locke proposed that thinking happened by association* when one idea led to another, and that in turn led to another. So thoughts were made up of chains of ideas, and new thoughts (as well as learning) occurred when we came to add new elements on to an existing chain.

SOMETHING TO TRY

A remarkable feature of our thought is its unpredictability. Look at the following words and write down the first word or idea that comes into your head.

cabbage	*prison*
pen	*World cup*
curtain	*Benidorm*
honesty	*next*
St Pancras Station	*star*

Look at your answers. They will be different to everyone else's answers to the same words. Try to work out why you made these associations.

Thinking as a response to biological demands

The psychoanalyst Sigmund Freud proposed that thinking arises from trying to find ways of satisfying our biological urges. The internal, biological need would produce an internal image of what would be needed to satisfy that need, and thinking would then take the form of a kind of problem solving, in which the main focus was to make that internal image into reality. So, for example, a

FIGURE 2. *Dreaming of food.*

toddler feeling hungry would have an internal image of what it wanted — food — and would begin to think in order to make that internal image real by obtaining real food.

✏️ SOMETHING TO TRY

Look at your associations in the previous activity again. Were they influenced at all by your 'biological urges'? For example, did the word curtain remind you of the curtains in a café? Was this because you were hungry?

Thinking as adaptation to the environment

The developmental psychologist Jean Piaget (1952) argued that thinking arises as part of the process of biological adaptation*. All organisms, he argued, adapt to their environment, and in the case of human infants, they do so by building up a model of the world in their minds. The model is built up from the experiences of the child, and it takes the form of frameworks (known as schemata*) which help to guide future actions as well as to make sense of experiences. These **schemata** develop continually, because they are added to by the child's inter-actions with the world; and since they provide a guide for actions, they help the child to adapt effectively.

Thinking as cognitive restructuring (figuring it out)

FIGURE 3. *Exercising control.*

The Russian psychologist Vygotsky (1962) argued that thought arises from the child's needs to *re*-structure situations cognitively — in other words, to work out how things could be different. The child perceives that things do not always stay the same, and it gradually learns that it can actually change some things in the world. Something as simple as pushing over a pile of bricks can be exciting to a young child because it demonstrates that they can have some control over their world. In Vygotsky's model, thinking develops as the child plans out the changes that it will make, or develops explan-ations for what is happening. It becomes more sophisticated once the child develops language.

3

Thinking as resolving discrepancies

Another view sees thinking as something which arises when our experience doesn't quite match up to our expectations. This view was put forward by Dewey, and is often known as the 'trouble' theory of thought. Dewey suggested that most of the time we act quite automatically and don't think about what we are doing much. But if we try to do something, and our experience doesn't fit what we expect, this poses a puzzle, and we will begin to think about it. So, for instance, you may take very little notice of what you are doing when you are getting dressed in the morning, but if you reach to take hold of a button and it is missing, you notice it because there is a discrepancy between what you expected and what actually happens. This discrepancy provokes you to think about it: 'How did I lose that button?'; or 'I remember now, it came off yesterday'.

As you can see, a number of different possible explanations have been suggested for how thinking develops. In the next few Parts, we will go on to look at some of the different aspects of thinking which have been studied by psychologists.

 SOMETHING TO TRY

Look back at the five different explanations of thinking that psychologists have given and try to think of one example of your thoughts today that fit into each category.

 (a) List the five approaches to thinking.

(b) What is cognitive restructuring?

(c) What does 'resolving discrepancies' refer to?

(d) What is thinking?

4

2 Reasoning

KEY AIMS: By the end of Part 2 you should:

▷ *understand the concept of reasoning*
▷ *be able to discuss the approaches used by psychologists to study human thought*
▷ *be able to explain some of the distinctions between human thinking and logical thinking.*

We often assume that people think logically*, building up their argument a piece at a time. In fact, much human thinking doesn't work in quite that way at all. Thouless, in 1974, showed how many of the common arguments used by politicians, the media, and people in everyday conversation contain logical errors, like non sequiturs (conclusions which don't follow from what has just been said); or the use of emotionally coloured words to influence the listener. But Thouless was identifying deliberate tricks of argument, which could be used by a skilled debater. In this Part, we will look at some other distinctive, but not necessarily logical, types of thinking which have been studied by psychologists.

 SOMETHING TO TRY

A local politician mounted an argument against sex education in schools. On local radio he argued that in the fifties we did not have sex education in schools, and also in the fifties there was less prostitution, venereal disease and fewer child pregnancies. Therefore, sex education caused venereal disease, etc.

Think of three examples yourself of arguments that contain logical errors. Try to think of a political argument, a personal argument and a medical or health argument.

Insight learning

One type of learning* which was studied quite extensively by the Gestalt* psychologists became known as insight* learning. This is the type of learning which you might have experienced when, all of a sudden, something falls into place, and you seem to grasp the answer very quickly. Some psychologists refer to this as the 'Aha!' experience, because that's what it feels like! In cartoon films a light bulb appears above the character's head.

FIGURE 4. *The insight light bulb.*

SOMETHING TO TRY

Think about an 'Aha!' experience that you have had recently. What was it? What happened? How did you feel?

One of the Gestalt psychologists, Wolfgang Köhler (1925), argued that it isn't just human beings who show insight learning. He performed a series of studies with captive chimpanzees, in which he posed them a number of puzzles which couldn't be solved through trial and error*. Instead, they could only be solved by the animal mentally restructuring the situation so as to grasp the solution to the problem.

Chimpanzee insight

For example, in one experiment, a chimpanzee was in its cage, and a piece of fruit was hung from the ceiling, out of reach. Around the cage were scattered several boxes, none of which was high enough on its own to allow the chimpanzee to reach the fruit. Köhler reported that the chimpanzee would make a few half-hearted attempts to reach the swinging fruit, and then give up. But after mooching around its cage for a while, it would suddenly begin to move purposefully, would pile a set of boxes on top of one another, and would climb on them to reach the fruit. It seemed that the solution to the problem had suddenly struck the animal — it had suddenly gained an insight into the problem.

FIGURE 5. *How to reach the bananas.*

There are other explanations for the behaviour of the chimps, however, and it has been found that chimps with prior experience of boxes showed 'insight' more readily. Also, some chimps would stack the boxes and climb up them even when there was no prize of a banana at the top. So although we might like to believe that animals have similar thought processes to ourselves, it would appear that the evidence is far from convincing.

Human beings, however, do quite often demonstrate a sudden insight into a problem, and the Gestalt psychologists saw this cognitive restructuring as being an important element in human thinking and learning, which should be taken into account by anyone trying to understand how people think.

SAQ 2

What are the differences between insight learning and trial-and-error learning?

Cognitive style

Liam Hudson (1966) performed an extensive study of schoolchildren, looking particularly at whether they had chosen 'arts' or 'science' subjects at school. He found that there seemed to be two different types of cognitive style* shown by pupils in the study, which he labelled as 'convergent'* and 'divergent' thinking*. Convergent thinkers tended to be extremely logical, to prefer science or mathematical subjects, and to adopt a linear, focused style of reasoning if they were asked to solve a particular problem. Divergent thinkers were often much more intuitive or impulsive in their style of thought, tended to prefer arts subjects at school, and would range widely across several possible options if they were asked to solve a problem. However, it has not always been possible to replicate these results which suggests that the process is more complex than suggested by Hudson.

Uses for a brick

One of the tests which Hudson used to distinguish between these two cognitive styles was to ask the schoolchildren to think of unusual uses for everyday objects. So, for example, he would ask them 'how many' uses can you think of for

FIGURE 6. Brick and cup.

a brick?', and they would have a set period of time to write down as many as they could think of. He found that divergent thinkers would tot up many more uses than convergent thinkers, often coming up with ideas which their more convergent colleagues regarded as quite bizarre.

 SOMETHING TO TRY

Try this problem yourself. How many uses can you think of for a brick and for a cup? Give yourself just two minutes for each object.

Human reasoning

One interesting aspect of research has concerned the ways that human beings reason. This research suggests that looking at human thinking as the simple, logical processing of information may be misleading; there are some systematic differences.

Processing negative statements

Wason showed that we find it much harder, and take longer, to process negative information than we do to process positive information. So people who are asked to comprehend a statement like:

'If the circle is red, then the triangle will be blue'

will do so more easily than they will comprehend a sentence like:

'If the circle is not brown, then the triangle will not be green'.

Although the two statements are logically equivalent, people take longer to process negative information and are more likely to make mistakes.

Probabilistic reasoning

Similarly, Wason and Johnson Laird (1970) showed that people tend to apply their broader knowledge of what is likely when they are solving problems, and this may also mean that they don't always reason according to strict formal logic. For example, if you heard your friend say: 'I'll go for a walk on Sunday if the weather is fine,' you would be likely also to conclude that she wouldn't go for a walk if it was raining. To a human being, that just seems reasonable. But to a computer, which operates by formal logic, there would be just as much chance of seeing your friend go for a walk in the rain as in the sunshine on that particular Sunday. Saying that 'I will do this if ...' is not the same as saying 'I won't do this if not'; in the same way, saying that 'all guitars are musical instruments' is not the same as saying 'all musical instruments are guitars'.

So human reasoning isn't quite the same thing as formal logic. Some psychologists have seen these features of the way that human beings think as 'errors' in reasoning, because they don't match up to strictly logical processes. But others see them as evidence that human reasoning is far more subtle and sophisticated, since it doesn't just include the elements of the problem, but also looks at its whole social context, taking into account prior knowledge about the world and about the probable actions of people.

Decision making

The issue of the difference between human reasoning and logic also affects psychological investigations of decision making. Most decisions require some evaluation followed by a choice of action. For example, shall I have a bowl of cereal for breakfast or some toast and Marmite? Shall I watch a documentary on the environment or shall I go to the pub? Some decisions are more difficult than others.

The research by psychologists has tended to concentrate on how we use probabilities to make decisions. An example that a psychologist might look at would be to examine the choice of subject to study at college. The choice might involve some consideration of the outcomes of that choice, for example, if I choose to study psychology, what is the probability of getting a job at the end of the course? The problem for psychologists is that a decision such as this is rarely based solely on logic or probabilities. The choice of subject to study is affected by a number of factors including: the choices that friends make, the self image of the student, the influence of parents, the influence of teachers, etc. These influences are hard to quantify and hard to fit into a logical model of decision making.

This problem of the differences between logical thinking and human thinking has meant that psychologists have often studied the 'errors' in human thinking compared to logical thinking. For example, Tversky and Kahneman (1974) described one common 'error' that people make when they are given probability problems to solve. In one problem in their study participants were told that an imaginary person called Linda is a former activist, single, very intelligent and a philosophy graduate. They were then asked to estimate the probabilities of her being a bank teller, a feminist, or a feminist bank teller. Most people said that it is more probable that she is a feminist bank teller than a bank teller. This cannot be correct because the category of bank tellers includes all feminist bank tellers.

There are numerous studies that highlight the differences between logical decision making and human decision making. This can be no surprise since it is clear that logic is not the major factor in decision making. We have to take into account social factors, past experience, emotions and, on some occasions, sheer devilment. People sometimes say, 'I know it's stupid, and I know it will probably end in failure, but I'm going to try anyway'. So, the area of human decision making is probably best explored by social psychologists rather than cognitive psychologists.

SAQ
3

(a) What are the differences between convergent and divergent thinking?

(b) What is probabilistic reasoning?

(c) What are the advantages of probabilistic reasoning over formal logic?

(d) What are the advantages of formal logic over probabilistic reasoning?

Representation

KEY AIMS: By the end of Part 3 you should:

▷ *be able to discuss the idea of mental representation*
▷ *be familiar with the various ways that we represent knowledge using mental processes*
▷ *be able to evaluate the different psychological approaches.*

One of the major interests of cognitive psychologists has been the question of how we represent information to ourselves, mentally. Obviously, we don't just take in information and store it haphazardly — otherwise how would we ever remember things at the right times? Clearly, we use some form of mental representation which helps us not only store factual information, but also to direct and guide our actions on the basis of our world knowledge and our previous experience.

Concept formation

One of the main ways that we store factual knowledge is by classifying it into concepts*, which allows us to handle much more information than we possibly could if we treated each new bit of information as if it were totally unique.

SOMETHING TO TRY

Look at the following faces. Your task is to put them into two groups.

FIGURE 7. *Faces.*

What characteristics did you use to group them?

Associationist models of concept formation

How we go about this classification is interesting, and several different mechanisms have been suggested. One of the first was put forward by Hull (1943), who argued that we link things together by association generalizing from one stimulus and responding in the same way to any other stimulus which has features in common with it. However, some psychologists criticized this idea on the grounds that concepts can't be formed simply by associating together things which had similar features, because sometimes things which belonged to the same category have very few features in common. For example, taking the concept 'chair', just how many features do an armchair and a three-legged stool have in common?

SOMETHING TO TRY

Try to define the word 'table'. It's not as easy as it seems. When you have a definition, try and think of examples of tables that do not fit in, and examples of other objects that do.

Rosch (1975) argued that 'natural' concepts (concepts which occur in everyday life, of objects and events that we experience) are linked not by particular sets of features, but by the actions which people undertake in relation to them. So the connection between an armchair and a stool occurs because both are things that you sit on. Moreover, in the case of 'natural' concepts of this kind, we operate on the basis of a kind of ideal 'prototype' which is typical of the concept. We link other things with the prototype if they show a kind of 'family resemblance', which might include usage. (See Figure 8.)

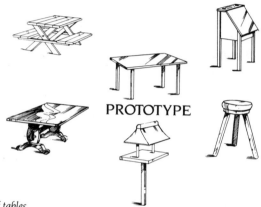

FIGURE 8. A *family of tables.*

Collins and Quillian (1969) investigated how concepts are stored in memory, and suggested that we store them according to some kind of hierarchical classification system. They timed how long it took people to say 'true' or 'false' to statements like 'a robin is a bird', or 'a shark is an animal'. When they analysed the results, they found that people took less time to respond to statements where the two categories were at similar levels (e.g. 'a robin has feathers'), and longer to respond to statements which linked lower and higher level categories (e.g. 'a blue jay is an animal'). (See Figure 9.) Further research has found that these findings are only replicable under certain circumstances. So, once again, we have to conclude that the process is more complex than Collins and Quillian suggest.

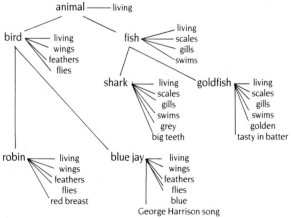

FIGURE 9. A *hierarchy of concepts. (After Collins and Quillian,* 1969.)

Schemas

Another type of representation is the schema. A schema is more than a concept because it is not just concerned with representing factual information, but also with directing future courses of action and organizing how we deal with it. Neisser (1976) suggested that we form some schemas, called anticipatory schemas, which are important in telling us how we should act in our environment. Our actions, in turn, mean that we sample our environment, noticing only certain things from amongst the wealth of information available to us at any given moment. It is this selection of information which, in turn, feeds and modifies our anticipatory schemata, allowing us to take our experiences into account in predicting what will occur next. Neisser saw this perceptual cycle as being the core to all cognition. Cognition, he says, occurs because we are active in the world and actively sampling it.

 SOMETHING TO TRY

Think about the street you live on. Try and sketch as much of it as you can, putting in any distinguishing features. On my street there is a pub and a number of shops. I walk down this street most days to get the bus. When I try to draw it, I find I have only noticed some aspects of it. Look at your sketch and compare it with your street. What have you left out? What have you drawn incorrectly? What have you drawn that isn't really there?

Rumelhart (1980) suggested that there are four ways of thinking about schemata, each of which has been adopted by different psychologists researching into that area.

(1) Schemata can be seen as plays containing information about characters, setting, and scripts for appropriate sequences of action.

(2) Schemata can be seen as theories, which allow us to produce a meaningful explanation for what is happening around us.

(3) Schemata can be seen as computer systems, allowing us to process information that we are receiving from the world.

(4) Schemata can be seen as decoders, breaking down and analysing the components of everyday living in the same way as a grammatical parser will break down a sentence into its grammatical parts and its meanings.

 SOMETHING TO TRY

If you have a video recorder, tape ten minutes of a drama show. Watch the show and then write down what happened in as much detail as you can. Now watch the ten minutes again and compare it with your description. You will find that you have made some errors, as you did in your description of your street. These errors will be caused, in part, by the schemas you use to structure your view of the world.

Scripts

In 1977, Schank and Abelson suggested that we live much of our everyday lives according to well defined and well understood 'scripts'*. These allow us to identify what is going on, and to know how we should act in order to be socially acceptable. The classic example of a script is the way that you know what to expect and how to behave when you go to a restaurant. Although nobody actually tells you, a very little experience is enough to tell you what is likely to happen. If anyone involved, for example, the waiter, or yourself, or your companion, were to begin to act in a very odd or different kind of way, the 'script' would be broken; but in practice this doesn't happen very often. There are 'scripts' for other everyday life situations too, like going to a disco, attending school, or catching a bus.

SOMETHING TO TRY

You realize how 'scripted' life is when you start to fluff your lines deliberately.

Try this next time you go to the doctor. Walk into the surgery, walk over to the desk, grab the doctor firmly by the hand and pat him or her on the shoulder. Look the doctor in the eye and say, in a strong voice, 'Good to see you again, Doc, how are you doing?' In any other place this might be appropriate behaviour, but not here.

On second thoughts, maybe you should try this as a role play — less fun, but safer.

Schank and Abelson suggested that scripts could be classified into three types:

(1) situational scripts, which involve the kind of typical social situations that I have just been describing;

(2) personal scripts, like the expectations and behaviours involved in being someone's friend;

(3) instrumental scripts, associated with particular targets or goals, like those to do with travelling home from school or college.

Cognitive maps

The idea of the cognitive map* was first suggested by Tolman, in 1948, who showed that even rats seemed to be able to develop a 'mental picture' of where they were, which helped them in getting to a particular goal when they were motivated to do so. In human terms, we use cognitive maps frequently and a number of researchers have shown how these maps often represent our personal involvement with the world. For example, Saarinen (1973) found that when college students were asked to draw a map of their campus, they tended to enlarge the areas which were most well known and important to them, and to underestimate the size of those areas which they didn't go into very much.

FIGURE 10. *Cognitive maps.*

13

SOMETHING TO TRY

You've already been asked to draw a map of your street. Now try a sketch map of your route to college or work. Put in the main features. Now look at a published map of the area and compare your cognitive map with the actual map.

Interestingly, though, an opposite effect seems to occur when we are judging distance. Briggs (1971) showed that people tend to underestimate the length of a well known journey, whereas when they were asked to estimate distances between two landmarks that they didn't know very well, they tended to over-estimate. You may have found this yourself: the first time you visit a place it often seems very large, or the distances seem very great; but as you become more familiar with it they seem to become smaller.

It is difficult to describe accurately how we represent ideas and objects in thought. This difficulty is partly because we have to use thought to describe thought. We have considered schemas, scripts and cognitive maps, and these different forms of representation are concerned with representing different types of information, although they may be linked in other ways. Some researchers, for example, see a script as being a special kind of schema; whereas other researchers (who are usually using a different definition of what a schema is) will hotly dispute this, and may even argue that the whole concept of 'schema' is too woolly to be of any use to anyone.

(a) *What are the following:*
— *schemas?*
— *scripts?*
— *cognitive maps?*

(b) *What are the factors that influence and distort our mental representation of the world?*

The Development of Representation

KEY AIMS: By the end of Part 4 you should:

▷ *be familiar with Bruner's modes of representation*

▷ *understand Piaget's approach to cognitive development.*

How do internal representations develop? We will look at two of the main approaches because this research can be valuable in showing us how information which has been stored in different ways can be put to use.

Modes of representation

J.S. Bruner, in 1957, proposed that there are developmental changes in the way that we use different *modes* of representation for different types of information.

Enactive representation

When we are small infants, we are tied to our immediate world and the actions which we can perform upon it, and so the mode by which we store information about that world is linked closely with muscular actions. It is hard to imagine how a baby thinks. It cannot think in pictures of objects because it has not really discovered what objects are yet, or what properties they have. It remembers things as a kind of 'muscle memory' using an internal representation of the 'feel' of things to code the information.

Iconic representation*

As the infant grows older, though, its world widens to include a number of things which are not easily coded using enactive representation. The same muscle actions are involved in looking at several different picture books, for instance. So a different mode of representation becomes important, one which stores information as visual images. Bruner called this iconic representation.

Symbolic representation*

Pretty soon, though, the child's world widens further still, until it includes information which isn't easily represented using pictures, either. Try imaging a concept like 'freedom' or 'fairness'. When this happens, the child becomes more likely to use symbolic representation, which involves using symbols to 'stand for' the information. We are able to use symbolic representation from quite an early age. After all, numbers are symbols of this sort, and most children learn the concept of 'fairness' quite early in their school years. But as a general rule, children tend to use the iconic mode, and then change to using the symbolic mode more when they enter adolescence. In fact, there is some evidence that our ability to visualize becomes less accurate after that point.

The flexibility of symbolic representation Symbolic representation has the advantage that it is much more flexible than iconic representation. In a study which illustrated this, Bruner and Kenney (1966) asked children to memorize a set of glasses placed on a grid pattern in ascending order of size (see Figure 11). There were two groups of children of the same age; one group which used

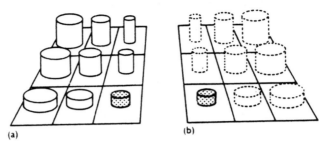

FIGURE 11. *Children from five to seven were shown the arrangement of glasses in (a), and, when it was dismantled, were able to reconstruct it. However, when the shaded glass was placed as in (b), and the children were asked to complete the pattern, only the older ones could do it. [After Bruner and Kenney, 1966. Reprinted by permission of Thomas Helson.]*

iconic representation and one which used symbolic representation. Although both were equally good at placing the glasses in the pattern that they had already seen, only those who used symbolic representation could replace them in reverse order when they were asked to do so. The iconic imagery used by the other group had given them such as inflexible image that they were unable to change it around mentally.

SOMETHING TO TRY

Try to use the different modes of representation.

(a) *Try and remember what it felt like the last time you went on the 'waltzer'. Remembering this sensation involves enactive representation.*

(b) *Now try and remember your bedroom. To do this you probably use iconic representation as you mentally look round the room. Strangely, it is usually tidier in your imagination than it is in real life.*

(c) *Place five pieces on a chess board and make a mental note of their position on the board. Now remove the pieces. Turn the board through 90°, and try and put the pieces back into their positions. To do this you have to rotate your mental images and use symbolic representation (though visual imagery could also be involved).*

Representation and revision strategies

One of the problems which some students encounter with revision, is that they are attempting to use revision strategies which they developed during childhood when their iconic representation was at its peak. But they continue to use such strategies long after the information that they are trying to learn has become inappropriate for these strategies. For example, it's quite surprising how many students try to revise by staring at a page of notes as if trying to 'fix' a visual image of them in the brain. They recall using that technique successfully in earlier years, and so they try to apply it to GCSE and A-level revision. But it doesn't work. For one thing, the information is more complex and there are many more pages than there used to be. And for another, at this level they need to understand and be able to manipulate the information, and we have seen that iconic representation doesn't encourage that. Revision strategies which help you to understand the material and change it around are much more effective when you are sixteen, no matter how good you were at visualizing when you were twelve.

FIGURE 12. *The puzzled student.*

The development of schemata

A different view of how representation develops was suggested by the developmental psychologist Jean Piaget. Piaget proposed that cognitive development occurs with the formation and building up of schemata. Piaget suggested that schemata are mental representations which serve as a guide to action, as well as containing information that we have learned. Piaget proposed that schemata are continually developing and changing throughout our lives, as we interact with our environment.

The body schema

According to Piaget, the first schema that the infant develops is its body schema*, when it first learns to separate the world into 'me' and 'not me'. From then on, its learning consists of developing and revising that schema, as it performs more operations on the outside world and learns from the effects that those operations have.

Assimilation

The way in which schemata develop, Piaget believed, was through the two processes of assimilation* and accommodation*. Through assimilation, a schema is extended to apply to a broader range of objects in the outside world. So the infant's 'drinking' schema, which might first apply only to milk, develops with the child's broader experience and comes to apply also to other liquids — orange juice, water, and the like. During the process of assimilation, the schema's area of reference is extended, but the schema itself doesn't change.

Accommodation

The second method by which schemata develop, according to Piaget, is known as accommodation. During accommodation, the schemata themselves have to change to 'fit' the incoming information. They may even subdivide, forming a completely new schema, if the new information is different enough from what was previously accepted. By continuously accommodating our increasing knowledge of the world, the first 'not me' schema of the infant becomes developed and extended into the very sophisticated forms of knowledge that the adult holds about the outside world.

For example, imagine a little girl learning her first few words. She can say four words; 'mama' = mummy, 'dada' = all men (very embarrassing this), 'ocolit' = sweeties, and 'teddie' = small furry things. When the little girl sees a duck for the first time, she doesn't say 'what's that, then?', but immediately identifies it as a 'teddie'. She has assimilated the duck into the existing schema of 'teddie'. As she perceives more features in the various objects in the 'teddie' schema, she eventually accommodates and develops new schema.

We can see, then, that both of these theories about the development of representation can tell us something about what is happening in later life. Adults as well as children may use different modes of representation, and the extension of schemata through assimilation and accommodation occurs just as much in adult life as in childhood.

SAQ
5

(a) *Describe the three modes of representation.*

(b) *What are 'assimilation' and 'accommodation'?*

Problem Solving

KEY AIMS: By the end of Part 5 you should:

▷ *be familiar with the various psychological approaches to problem solving*

▷ *be familiar with the advantages and disadvantages of the various methods.*

There have been many studies of how we go about solving problems. What emerges from the research is how powerful learned associations and habits of thought can become — so much so, in fact, that they can often limit our success in tackling new situations.

SOMETHING TO TRY

1. *You decide to take your dog for a walk in the country. You put the dog into your car and head off. Unfortunately, when you arrive in the country, you inadvertently lock your keys in the car. What would you do?*

2. *You are out for the evening with someone you are trying to impress. Unfortunately, when you go to the toilet you break the zip in your dress/trousers. What do you do?*

How do you solve these everyday problems? What are your solutions to these problems? How did you arrive at them? Now read what psychologists have investigated in this area of problem solving and see how your methods match up.

Trial-and-error learning

Some of the very earliest studies of problem solving were performed by E.L. Thorndike (1898), who investigated the way that cats learned to escape from a 'puzzle box' through trial-and-error learning. The hungry cat was shut into a small box and food was placed outside. Dangling from the ceiling of the box was a string, and if it was pulled, the front of the box would open so that the cat could escape. Thorndike timed how long it took each cat to escape from the box each time it was shut in, and found that the time taken gradually became less and less as the cat had more experiences of solving the puzzle successfully. Through trial and error, it gradually learned to associate pulling the string with escaping from the box.

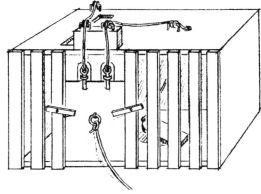

FIGURE 13. *Thorndike's puzzle box.* (From E.L. Thorndike, **Animal Intelligence.** New York, Macmillan Publishing Co., 1911.)

Learning sets

In 1949, H.F. Harlow proposed that such trial-and-error learning could generalize into what he described as a 'learning set'*. The word 'set' here means much the same as it means when the starter of a race says 'get ready, get set, go'; it means a state of readiness, or preparedness. Harlow gave rhesus monkeys a series of 'odd one out' problems, which they learned to solve for a reward. They were presented with three objects, two similar, one different. If the monkey picked up the one that was different from the others, it would find a raisin or a peanut underneath it.

Harlow showed that the monkeys were not simply learning to respond to a specific stimulus, because once they had had several exposures to the problem, they seemed to grasp the concept of 'oddness', and would choose a correct 'odd' object even if it had represented a 'wrong' answer on the trial before. Instead, he argued, the monkeys had developed a learning set, which meant that they were ready to solve that type of problem, regardless of the specific stimulus which constituted it.

Mental sets

Human beings can also develop mental sets* in this way. Luchins (1959) showed how enough experience of a particular way of solving one type of problem meant that people would tend to choose that solution even if there was an easier and quicker way of solving the problem. Although sometimes a mental set means that we can find solutions quickly, it can also blind us to alternative possibilities, so that we repeatedly choose that one kind of solution.

Einstellung

The Gestalt psychologists called this tendency for thinking to become fixed, or set, Einstellung*. They argued that, partly because of their tendency to develop mental sets, and partly because of particular characteristics of human thinking, people could become reluctant to accept new ideas or new ways of tackling a problem.

The principle of closure

One of the characteristics of human thought which the Gestalt psychologists identified as sometimes causing problems in this way is known as the principle of closure. This refers to the way that we tend to look for completeness in things that we see, so if we are presented with disconnected stimuli, we will tend to look for a way to join them up into a meaningful figure by filling in the missing bit. For instance, we see the shape in Figure 14 as a broken triangle, rather than simply as a set of lines. This principle can mean that we become very easily tricked by assuming that there

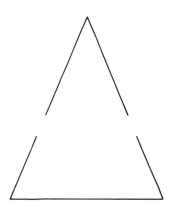

FIGURE 14. *Closure.*

are boundaries or limits to problems, which don't really exist. The difficulty many people have in solving the nine dot problem (Figure 15), the first time they see it, is an example of this.

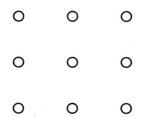

Join up all the dots with four straight lines, without going over the same line twice or taking the pen off the paper.

FIGURE 15. *9 dot problem*.

Functional fixedness

Another kind of Einstellung occurs when we are unable to think of ways to use objects outside of their normal function. This is known as functional fixedness*, and can mean that we fail to find solutions to some kinds of problem because it doesn't occur to us that we can use items for other than their normal function. Glucksberg (1962) asked participants to mount two small candles on to a wall. They were provided with the two candles, a box of matches, and a few drawing pins; and Glucksberg found that many of the people couldn't solve the problem, because it involved using the materials in unexpected ways. Being highly motivated didn't help either; in fact it seemed to make the functional fixedness worse, if anything. When participants were offered a $20 reward for solving the problem, they performed even less well than those who hadn't been offered any reward. Can you work out the solution?

FIGURE 16. *Functional fixedness.*

Lateral thinking

There have been a number of efforts made to teach people how too break free from these kinds of limitations to their thinking. De Bono (1969) developed a training course to teach people what he described as lateral thinking* — the ability to step outside the boundaries of a problem and to develop innovative and novel solutions. De Bono's approach involved deliberately trying to identify the assumed or taken for granted limitations to problem solving, and approaching the problem in a completely new way, as if nothing like it had ever been encountered before.

SOMETHING TO TRY

*In his book, **Children Solve Problems** (1972), Edward De Bono presents a range of responses from children to unusual problems. Try and think of some solutions to the problem of how to stop a dog and cat from fighting.*

Brainstorming

Another technique which is often used in creative areas like marketing and advertizing to develop new ideas and to get away from the restrictions of mental sets and assumptions is known as brainstorming. This technique has three stages. In the first stage, a group of people get together and generate as many ideas as they can about a particular topic. At this point, nobody tries to be practical, and no idea is rejected; everything is noted down for consideration later, no matter how crazy or silly it might seem. This is important; otherwise people find it hard to generate ideas. Later, when the flow of ideas dries up, the group moves on to the second stage, in which they look at the list and reject any which are obviously impractical or irrelevant. Then they go through the remaining possibilities, and discuss how each one might work in practice. Brainstorming is a very useful technique for getting novel solutions to problems, and the freedom of the first stage means that completely new ideas can come up which were undreamt of before the session started.

FIGURE 17. *Brainstorming.*

We can see, then, that studies of how people (and some animals) go about solving problems presents us with quite a lot of information about the influence of mental sets. In the next Part, we will look at how psychologists have used computers to investigate some different aspects of problem solving and thinking.

SOMETHING TO TRY

Think about the following everyday problems. What do you think is the best method to tackle them?

(a) How to stop a colleague from making offensive jokes.

(b) How to think of a different birthday present for Granny.

(c) How to pass your examinations.

(a) Some problem-solving techniques narrow and others expand the range of answers. Make a list of those that narrow, and a list of those that expand the range of possible answers to a problem.

(b) What are the advantages of techniques that narrow the range of possible answers?

(c) What are the advantages of techniques that expand the range of possible answers?

6 Computer Modelling

KEY AIMS: By the end of Part 6 you should:

▷ *be familiar with the concept of computer simulation*

▷ *be familiar with the various ways that psychologists have explored computer models of mental processes*

▷ *be able to evaluate these approaches to human thought.*

During the 'cognitive revolution' of the 1960s and 1970s, many psychologists adopted the viewpoint that the human brain acted as an information processor, in other words, it operated like a highly complicated computer. This idea led in turn to the question of whether using computers might help us in finding out more about problem solving.

Computer simulation

Some research into this area concentrated on using computers to simulate how human beings think, in the hope that by doing so, we can learn more about the human brain. This area of research is generally referred to as computer simulation.

 SOMETHING TO TRY

Try to develop three lists. First write down as many cognitive skills as you can that both people and computers have. Then, write down as many things as you can that computers can do that people cannot do. Finally, write down as many cognitive skills as you can that people have and computers haven't.

The General Problem Solver

One of the first attempts at computer simulation was developed by Newell and Simon, in 1972. The General Problem Solver, or GPS, as it became known, involved comparing how things are at the beginning of the problem, the initial state, with how things would be when the problem had been solved — the goal state. The difference between the two is known as the problem space.

In this model, the best way of solving the problem is to think of it in terms of reducing the problem space. But the problem space might be quite large, even in the simplest problems, and exploring all of the possibilities will be cumbersome. So Newell and Simon proposed that, instead of using an algorithm (a method which looks at all of the possible steps in the whole problem and works out what the consequences of each one would be) the problem is better approached using means-end analysis.

Means-end analysis

Means-end analysis* involves breaking the problem down into a number of smaller stages, or sub goals, which will serve to reduce the problem space. Once these sub goals have been identified, the problem solver takes the step which

23

will reach the first sub goal, and the problem space is then recalculated. Then the step which leads towards the next sub goal is identified and taken, and so on.

This is known as a heuristic* approach. Heuristics are choices which are made because they look as though they are likely to produce the right effect — in this case, to reduce the problem distance. Adopting a heuristic strategy means that we are more likely to solve the problem efficiently. Heuristics can be very useful as 'short cuts' to solving problems. But, of course, they can go wrong, too, because they can sometimes mean that we ignore alternative possibilities in much the same way as the development of a mental 'set' may mean that we don't consider fully what other options are available.

 SOMETHING TO TRY

Imagine you are standing in the middle of one town, say Nottingham, and you want to get to the middle of another town, say the Bull Ring in Birmingham. What are the sub goals of this problem?

Protocol analysis

Another approach in computer simulation is known as protocol analysis*. Protocols are steps taken in solving a problem, and using this method, people are asked to 'think out loud' as they tackle a problem, so that the researchers can identify the stages that they are using. Then these stages can be imitated in developing computer programs.

As you might imagine, though, this is a fairly controversial technique: what people say may not represent what they actually do; not because they are trying to fool the investigators, but because they may not be aware of it, or they may find it difficult to put into words. Often people's introspections are justifications for what they've done, rather than reasons why they did it.

That doesn't mean that the technique is useless, though. Ericsson and Simon (1984) argue that protocol analysis can be useful, as long as two conditions are met:

(1) if the person is describing what they are doing at that moment, rather than what they did previously; and

(2) if what the person is saying is also reflected in their actual behaviour, so that observers can see how the two things correlate.

 SOMETHING TO TRY

Try to say out loud what you are thinking, and what you intend to do while you are driving. If you haven't got a car, do it on your bike. Once you've had a go at this, think about how useful the method of protocol analysis is. (On second thoughts, it might be safer to choose an activity like playing croquet.)

Artificial Intelligence

A considerable amount of research has also aimed to produce computer systems which might aid or improve how human beings tackle problems. These attempts fall into the general category of artificial intelligence*.

Interactive programmes

One of the most famous attempts to produce a simulation of human thinking was a therapeutic program known as ELIZA. This program was an interactive one, in which a person sat at a keyboard and typed in questions, and the computer was programmed to respond as if it were the therapist. Although the computer was simply programmed to respond to certain stimulus words, people often reacted to ELIZA as if they were talking to a real person, and would become very involved in 'discussing' their personal problems. In some cases, participants announced that talking with ELIZA had been sufficient 'therapy', and they did not need to see a human therapist.

FIGURE 18. *Eliza has a problem too.*

Another interactive program of this kind was developed by Abelson, in 1976, whose program involved a series of statements and principles taken from the views expressed by a right wing American politician. By following the 'rules' which had been programmed into it, and also (like ELIZA) using key words to trigger off appropriate responses, the program was able to draw inferences from information which it was given, and it frequently produced novel responses that were almost identical to those expressed by the original politician himself.

Expert systems

Another interesting area of research is that into expert systems*. Computer programs have been developed which act as an additional database, designed to assist an expert in making professional decisions by providing easy access to extra information.

An expert system has to have three components:

(1) a knowledge base, providing information which is specific to the task and presented in a way that the expert can easily understand;

(2) some kind of system for looking at the available data and matching it up with the knowledge base (often referred to as an 'inference engine');

25

(3) a 'user friendly' interface, which allows the expert to communicate requests to it clearly and simply.

FIGURE 19. *The user friendly computer.*

One of the main problems which people encounter when they are trying to develop a computer expert system is the way that human experts often have implicit knowledge, which is not easily verbalized, and is, therefore, difficult to include in the database. Also, human experts can cover a wide range of questions, and can generalize from previous cases by recognizing general patterns, even when the particular elements of the case are not the same. For these reasons, it is unlikely that computer systems on their own could ever come to replace a human expert; but they can provide a professional with considerable assistance and detailed knowledge.

We can see, then, that research using computers has been useful in looking at problem solving generally, even though such research has its limitations.

SOMETHING TO TRY

Look back at your lists of cognitive skills displayed by computers and by people. What do you think are the differences between the way a computer thinks and the way people think? Or to put it another way, Commander Spock is First Officer on the 'USS Enterprise', and has the mind of a computer, but the Captain (James T Kirk) is in control of the vessel. Why will Spock never command the Enterprise?

SAQ
7

(a) *What is the General Problem Solver?*

(b) *What are protocols?*

(c) *What do you understand by the concept of Artificial Intelligence?*

ASSIGNMENTS

❏ Describe and evaluate attempts by psychologists to explain how we solve problems.

❏ Describe and evaluate psychological descriptions of human thought.

❏ What are the similarities and differences between human thought and computer thought?

FURTHER READING

CLAXTON, G. (1988) *Growth Points in Cognition*. London: Routledge. [A set of chapters by major figures in the field and summarizing whole areas of current research in cognitive psychology.]

EYSENCK, M. and KEENE, M. (1990) A *Student's Handbook of Cognitive Psychology*. Hove: Lawrence Erlbaum. [A useful and comprehensive survey of the current state of cognitive psychology including recent research, but not much about the historical development of the subject.]

HAYES, N. and ORRELL, S. (1987) *Psychology: An introduction*. Harlow: Longman. [Contains several chapters which outline basic theory and evidence in cognitive psychology, although not up-to-date research.]

JOHNSON-LAIRD, P. (1988) *The Computer and the Mind: An introduction to cognitive science*. London: Fontana. [A lucid introduction to basic approaches and recent research in cognitive science.]

MATLINE, M. (1983) *Cognition*. London: Holt, Rinehart & Winston. [A textbook which explains basic cognitive processes clearly and thoroughly. Highly recommended.]

STERNBERG, R. and SMITH, E. (1988) *The Psychology of Human Thought*. Cambridge: Cambridge University Press. [Contains overviews of what is known about, and currently being discovered about induction, deduction, causality, general problem solving, etc.]

STRATTON, P. and HAYES, N. (1988) A *Student Dictionary of Psychology*. London: Edward Arnold. [A useful aid to study, especially in cognitive psychology which contains a lot of specialist terminology.]

TAYLOR, I. and HAYES, N. (1990) *Investigating Psychology*. Harlow: Longman. [A resource book containing 100 short readings, exercises, questions and other material useful for the student studying at home, or for classwork. Includes chapters on cognition, research skills and effective study skills.]

THOULESS, R. (1974) *Straight and Crooked Thinking* (3rd Ed). London: Pan. [An invaluable guide to logical errors and pitfalls in argument based on the psychology of thinking.]

REFERENCES

Students studying psychology at pre-degree level, whether in schools, FE colleges or evening institutes, seldom have access to a well-stocked academic library; nor is it expected that they will have consulted all the original references. For most purposes, the books recommended in Further Reading will be adequate. This list is included for the use of those planning a full-scale project on this topic, and also for the sake of completeness.

ABELSON, R.P. (1976) Script processing in attitude formation and decision-making. In J.S. Carroll and J.W. Payne (Eds.) *Cognition and Social Behaviour* Hillsdale, NJ: Erlbaum.

BRIGGS, R. (1971) Urban Cognitive Distances. In M. Marlin, *Cognition* London: Holt Rinehart & Winston.

BRUNER, J.S. (1957) On perceptual readiness. *Psychological Review*, 64, 123-151.

BRUNER, J.S. and KENNEY, A. (1966) Unpublished study described in J.S. Bruner (1966) *Towards a Theory of Instruction.* Cambridge: Harvard University Press.

COLLINS, A.M. and QUILLIAN, M.R. (1969) Retrieval time from semantic memory. *Journal of Verbal Learning and Verbal Behaviour*, 8, 240-247.

DE BONO, E. (1969) *The Mechanism of Mind.* Harmondsworth: Penguin.

ERICSSON, K.A. and SIMON, H.A. (1984) *Protocol Analysis: Verbal reports as data.* Massachusetts: Bradford Books.

GLUCKSBERG, S. (1962) The influence of strength of drive on functional fixedness and perceptual recognition. *Journal of Experimental Psychology*, 63, 36-41.

HARLOW, H.F. (1949) The formation of learning sets. *Psychological Review*, 56, 51-65.

HUDSON, L. (1966) *Contrary Imaginations: A psychological study of the English schoolboy.* Harmondsworth: Penguin.

HULL, C.L. (1943) *Principles of Behaviour.* New York: Appleton-Century-Crofts.

KÖHLER, W. (1925) *The Mentality of Apes.* New York: Harcourt Brace.

LUCHINS, A.S. (1959) Primacy-recency in impression formation. In C.I. Hovland (Ed.) *The Order of Presentation in Persuasion.* New Haven: Yale University Press.

NEISSER, U. (1976) *Cognition and Reality.* San Francisco: W.H. Freeman.

NEWELL, A. and SIMON, H.A. (1972) *Human Problem Solving.* Englewood-cliffs, NJ: Prentice-Hall.

PIAGET, J. (1952) *The Origins of Intelligence in Children.* New York: International Universities Press.

ROSCH, E.H. (1975) Cognitive representations of semantic categories. *Journal of Experimental Psychology*, 104, 192-233.

RUMELHART, D.E. (1980) Schemata: the building blocks of cognition. In R. Spiro, B. Bruce and W. Brewer (Ed.) *Theoretical issues in reading comprehension.* Hillsdale, NJ: Erlbaum.

SAARINEN, T.F. (1973) The use of projective techniques in geographic research. In W.H. Ittelson (Ed.) *Environment and Cognition.* New York: Seminar Press.

SCHANK, R. and ABELSON, R. (1977) *Scripts, Plans, Goals and Understanding: An enquiry into human knowledge.* Hillsdale, NJ: Erlbaum.

THORNDIKE, E.L. (1898) Animal intelligence: an experimental study of the associative processes in animals. *The Psychological Review, Monograph Supplements* 2, No. 4.

THOULESS, R.H. (1974) *Straight and Crooked Thinking* (3rd Edn.) London: Pan.

TOLMAN, E.C. (1948) *Purposive Behaviour in Animals and Man.* New York: Appleton-Century-Crofts.

TVERSKY, A. and KAHNEMANN, D. (1974) Judgement under uncertainty: heuristics and biases. *Science*, 185, 1124-1131.

VYGOTSKY, L.S. (1962, orig. pub. 1934) *Thought and Language.* New York: Wiley.

WASON, P.C. and JOHNSON-LAIRD, P.N. (1970) A conflict between selecting and evaluating information in an inferential task. *British Journal of Psychology*, 61, 509-515.

GLOSSARY [Terms in bold type also appear as a separate entry]

Accommodation: in Piagetian theory, the process by which a schema, or cognitive structure, becomes adjusted to new information by extending or changing its form.

Adaptation: the process of adjusting to the environment in such a way that the maximum benefit can be obtained from it. Piaget uses the term for the processes whereby cognitive structures are made to correspond to reality.

Artificial Intelligence: computers performing tasks which previously required the application of human intelligence.

Assimilation: one of the two processes by which a **schema**, in Piagetian theory, is considered to develop. New information is said to be assimilated when it is fitted into existing schemata and so can be understood in relation to earlier learning.

Association: the linking of one thing to another in sequence.

Attention: the focusing of perception leading to an increased awareness of a limited range of stimuli.

Body schema: the internal representation which the individual has of their own body. According to Piaget, the very first schema formed by the infant develops from the first 'me/not me' distinction.

Cognitive: a term used to refer to 'higher' mental processes such as thinking, perceiving and remembering.

Cognitive map: an internal representation of a specific or general area which forms a plan or outline that can guide behaviour.

Cognitive style: distinctive patterns of cognition that characterize an individual, for example, **convergent thinking**.

Concept: a set of ideas and properties that can be used to group things together.

Convergent thinking: problem solving which works consistently towards a defined solution; a way of thinking that assumes there is a single right answer, and the best way to reach it is to work directly towards it.

Divergent thinking: thought which ranges around a problem to look for novel solutions.

Einstellung: a term used by Gestalt psychologists to refer to the kinds of **mental sets** which can influence problem solving by inducing a rigidity of thought which precludes the perception of alternative strategies or solutions.

Enactive representation: according to Bruner, the first mode of representation developed by the young child. It involves the storing of information in the form of kinaesthetic sensations, such as the way most adults would recall the sensation of a fairground waltzer or helter-skelter.

Expert systems: knowledge-based computer systems which are capable of limited decision making based on prior input from a number of human experts.

Functional fixedness: a form of **mental set** in which the individual is unable to deviate from using objects in a manner consistent with their normal functioning.

Gestalt psychology: Gestalt psychology emphasises the holistic nature of human experience and opposes the stimulus-response approach on the grounds that 'the whole is greater than the sum of the parts'.

Heuristics: problem-solving strategies which involve taking the most probable options from a possible set rather than working systematically through all possible alternatives.

Iconic representation: Bruner's second mode of representation refers to the use of mental imagery.

Insight: in learning, insight refers to the sudden and complete realization of a problem.

Lateral thinking: an approach to problem solving expounded by De Bono (1969) in which the aim is to move outside the immediate boundaries of the problem and to challenge unspoken assumptions.

Learning: a relatively permanent change in behaviour, knowledge or understanding that results from experience.

Learning sets: a generalized style of learning, or state of preparedness to solve problems in certain ways, which has been acquired through experience with similar types of problems.

Logic: a set of rules by which conclusions can be reliably deduced from initial statements.

Means-end analysis: an approach to problem solving that involves starting by specifying two things; (a) what the situation is to begin with, and (b) what is the ultimate goal of the problem.

Mental set: a state of preparedness to perform certain kinds of mental operations rather than others.

Protocol analysis: looking at a plan of the steps and stages involved in the solution of a problem.

Schema, schemata: a hypothetical model of the way information is stored. It is used to direct action and to understand the relationships between events. A schema would include all of the information relating to a particular event or type of event, including representations of previous actions, theoretical and practical knowledge about the event, ideas and opinions about it, etc.

Scripts: well established plans and outlines used to direct behaviour and to predict the behaviour of others in familiar circumstances. It includes conventional speech exchanges like the following which appears to be almost 'scripted': 'How are you today?', 'I'm fine, thanks, and you?'

Symbolic representation: the third mode of representation described by Bruner, in which information is stored as symbols, such as numbers, words or signs.

Thinking: a general term which can be defined in several different ways: (a) the use of symbolic processes, (b) any chain or series of ideas, or (c) ideation, the sequence of producing ideas concerned with the solving of specific problems or incongruities in models of reality. Thinking is usually taken to mean conscious cognition to the exclusion of unconscious processes.

Trial-and-error learning: learning which takes place as a result of trying out a variety of responses to a given stimulus, and repeating the responses that lead to positive outcomes.

29

ANSWERS TO SELF-ASSESSMENT QUESTIONS

SAQ 1 (a) The five approaches to thinking are:
— association
— a response to biological demands
— adaptation
— cognitive restructuring
— resolving discrepancies.

(b) Cognitive restructuring means working out, mentally, how things could be different.

(c) 'Resolving discrepancies' refers to the thinking that arises when our experience does not match up to our expectations.

(d) Thinking is a general term which can be defined in several different ways: (1) the use of symbolic processes (2) any chain or series of ideas (3) ideation; the sequence of producing ideas concerned with the solving of specific problems or incongruities in models of reality.

Thinking is usually taken to mean conscious cognition to the exclusion of unconscious processes.

SAQ 2 Insight learning involves the mental evaluation of a problem and a sudden mental solution. Trial-and-error learning, on the other hand, involves a series of actions of which only a few will be successful.

SAQ 3 (a) Convergent thinking is problem solving which works consistently towards a defined solution; a way of thinking that assumes there is a single right answer, and the best way to reach it is to work directly towards it.

Divergent thinking is thought which ranges around a problem to look for novel solutions.

(b) Probabilistic reasoning is the application of a broader knowledge of likely outcomes to the judgement of situations and events.

(c) The advantages of probabilistic reasoning over formal logic are that it is more subtle and sophisticated since it doesn't just include the elements of the problem, but also looks at the whole social context.

(d) The advantages of formal logic over probabilistic reasoning are accuracy and precision.

SAQ 4 (a) A schema is a hypothetical model of the way information is stored. It is used to direct action and to understand the relationships between events. A schema would include all of the information relating to a particular event or type of event, including representations of previous actions, theoretical and practical knowledge about the event, ideas and opinions about it, etc.

Scripts are well-defined and understood patterns of speech and behaviour that appear to be as rigid as the script of a play.

A cognitive map is an internal representation of a specific or general area which forms a plan or outline that can guide behaviour.

(b) The factors that influence and distort our mental representation of the world are:
— social relationships
— emotions
— expectations
— hopes
— attitudes
— self esteem
— biological states, for example, arousal level
— gender
— background
— motivation.

SAQ 5 (a) The three modes of representation are:
— Enactive mode: according to Bruner, the first mode of representation developed by the young child. It involves the storing of information in the form of kinaesthetic sensations, such as the way most adults would recall the sensation of a fairground waltzer or helter-skelter.
— Iconic mode: Bruner's second mode of representation refers to the use of mental imagery.
— Symbolic mode: the third mode of representation described by Bruner, in which information is stored as symbols, such as numbers, words or signs.

(b) Assimilation: One of the two processes by which a schema, in Piagetian theory, is considered to develop. New information is said to be assimilated when it is fitted into existing schema and so can be understood in relation to earlier learning.

Accommodation: In Piagetian theory, the process by which a schema, or cognitive structure, becomes adjusted to new information by extending or changing its form.

SAQ 6 (a) Problem-solving techniques:
Those which narrow the range of answers are:
— learning sets
— mental sets
— Einstellung
— functional fixedness.
Those which expand the range of answers are:
— trial-and-error learning
— lateral thinking
— brainstorming.

(b) The main advantage of techniques that narrow the range of possible answers is to obtain a simple answer quickly — most useful for simple problems or logical problems.

(c) The main advantage of techniques that expand the range of possible answers is to obtain a range of possible answers including novel ones.

SAQ 7 (a) The General Problem Solver is one of the first attempts at computer simulation developed by Newell and Simon. It involves using means-end analysis.

(b) Protocols are the steps and stages involved in the solution of a problem.

(c) Artificial Intelligence refers to computer systems which can 'reason', and which are used to produce models of human thinking.